FAMILY FARE 2
SUMMER COOKING
DELIA SMITH

D1827648

British Broadcasting Corporation

Published by the British Broadcasting Corporation
35 Marylebone High Street, London W1M 4AA
ISBN 0 563 12670 1
First published 1974
© Delia Smith 1974

Printed in Great Britain by
Lowe & Brydone (Printers) Ltd, Thetford, Norfolk

Contents

Introduction   5

Summer Fruits   7
    Summer Pudding, Pavlova, Orange Cheesecake with
    Strawberries

Salads   11
    Green Salad, Tomato Salad, New Potato Salad with
    Mint and Chives, Rice Salad, Salad Niçoise, Hot
    Herb and Garlic Loaf

Salad Dressings   17
    Homemade Mayonnaise, English Salad Sauce,
    Vinaigrette, Chicken Salad with Tarragon and Green
    Grapes

English Lamb   22
    Lamb Baked with Butter and Herbs, Gravy,
    Redcurrant, Orange and Mint Jelly, Mustard
    Glazed Lamb Chops or Cutlets

Fresh Salmon   25
    Fresh Salmon, Avocado Sauce, Cucumber and Soured
    Cream Sauce, Salmon Coulibiac

Summer Soups   30
    Gazpacho, Chilled Cucumber Soup, Homemade
    Tomato Soup

Summer Entertaining (1)   34
    Poached Trout with Herbs, Rhubarb Fool,
    Gooseberry Fool

Summer Entertaining (2)   37
    Duck with Cherries, Morello Cherry Sauce, Braised
    Peas with Lettuce and Spring Onion

Picnic Food   39
    Meat Loaf, Banana and Walnut Cake

Quiches and Tarts   42
    Cream, Bacon and Onion Tart, English Custard Tart

Egg Dishes   45
    Omelette Savoyarde, Florentine Eggs, Piperade

Spare Parts Cooking   49
    Kidneys in Fresh Tomato Sauce, Liver in Soured
    Cream Sauce, Kidneys in Jacket Potatoes

Pâtés   52
    Country Pâté, Rillettes de Tours (Pork Pâté)

Summer Extras

Old English Summer Soup, Tomato and Chilli Sauce,
Navarin of Lamb, New Potatoes with Mint and
Chives, Fresh Salmon and Cucumber Mousse,
Mackerel with Green Gooseberry Sauce, Beef braised
in White Wine, Raspberry Shortcake, Plum and Soured
Cream Flan, Wheatmeal Bread

Introduction

I've always believed that, very often, the best sort of cooking is the simplest. Home cooking lovingly prepared from the best ingredients available is, to my mind, infinitely preferable to long-drawn-out recipes that take up a great deal of time and patience. So many people who are willing to spend hours producing something spectacular never really learn to do the ordinary things well. And everyday things are what family cooking is all about.

In the last series of *Family Fare* I tried to show a cross-section of family dishes which beginners to cooking could take in their stride but which, at the same time, offered new or alternative ideas to more experienced cooks.

The only difference in this second series of *Family Fare* is that, whereas previously we were concerned with autumn and winter recipes, this time we have moved on to summer and the great variety of cooking it brings. It is, and always has been, part of my culinary philosophy to follow Nature closely and make the utmost of the changing seasons.

I hope you and your families enjoy cooking and eating the recipes in this series as much as – to judge from your kind letters – you did the previous ones. And may I here say thank you for those letters, which were so encouraging?

Summer Fruits

The only quarrel I have with Nature is that our delicious native summer fruits seem suddenly to appear all at once – market stalls are loaded with ripe strawberries, raspberries, cherries, redcurrants and blackcurrants, not to mention juicy peaches, apricots, green gooseberries and deep-red sun-ripened rhubarb stalks. So this is a hectic time for cooks, who'll be busy stocking freezers, and making fruit jams and endless pies, tarts and puddings. There are so many delectable sweet dishes to be made from summer fruits that it's very difficult to select favourites. Anyway, here are some of mine.

Summer Pudding
(serves 6)

1 lb raspberries
$\frac{1}{2}$ lb redcurrants
$\frac{1}{4}$ lb blackcurrants
1$\frac{1}{2}$-pint pudding basin lightly buttered

5 oz castor sugar
7–8 medium slices white bread (from a large loaf)

First of all the fruit must be prepared. Separate the redcurrants and blackcurrants from their stalks by holding the tip of the stalk firmly between finger and thumb and sliding the stalk between the prongs of a fork – pushing the fork downwards so pulling off the berries as it goes. Rinse all the fruits, picking out any raspberries that look at all musty.

Place the fruits with the sugar in a large saucepan over a medium heat and let them cook for about three to five minutes, only until the sugar has melted and the juices begin to run – don't overcook and so spoil the fresh flavour. Now remove the fruit from the heat, and line a 1$\frac{1}{2}$-pint pudding basin with the slices of bread, overlapping them and sealing well by pressing the edges together. Fill in any gaps with small pieces of bread, so that no juice can get through.

Pour the fruit in (except for a cupful of juice), and cover the pudding with another slice of bread. Then place a small plate or saucer (one that will fit exactly inside the rim of the bowl) on top, and on top of that place a 3-lb or 4-lb weight, and leave in the refrigerator overnight. Just before serving the pudding, turn it out on to a large serving dish and spoon the reserved juice all over, to soak any bits of bread that still look white. Serve cut into slices, with a bowl of thick cream on the table.

Pavlova
(serves 6)

3 large fresh egg whites	$\frac{3}{4}$ lb soft fruits
6 oz castor sugar	(raspberries, straw-
1 level teaspoon cornflour	berries and redcurrants
$\frac{1}{2}$ teaspoon vinegar	mixed)
$\frac{1}{2}$ pint whipped cream	A little icing-sugar

Pre-heat the oven to gas mark 2, 300°F. First prepare a baking sheet by oiling it lightly, then line it with grease-proof paper (which should also be oiled lightly). Place the egg whites in a large clean bowl and have the sugar measured and ready. Now whisk the egg whites until they form soft peaks and you can turn the bowl upside down without them sliding out (it's very important, though, not to over-beat the eggs because, if you do, they will start to collapse).

When they're ready, start to whisk the sugar in approximately 1 oz at a time, whisking after each addition, and when all the sugar is in whisk in the vinegar and cornflour. Now take a metal tablespoon and spoon the meringue mixture on to the prepared baking sheet, forming a circle of about eight inches in diameter. Make a round depression in the centre then, using the tip of a skewer, make little swirls in the meringue all round, lifting the skewer up sharply each time to leave tiny peaks.

Now place the baking sheet in the oven, then immediately turn the heat down to gas mark 1 (275°F) and leave it to cook for one hour. Then turn the heat right out but *leave* the Pavlova inside the oven until it's completely cold – I always find it's best to make a Pavlova in the evening and leave it in the turned-off oven overnight to dry out. It's my belief that the secret of successful meringues of any sort is to let them dry out completely, which is what this method does perfectly.

To serve the Pavlova, lift it from the baking sheet, peel off the paper and place it on a serving dish. Then just before serving, spread the whipped cream on top, arrange the raspberries, etc., on top of the cream and dust with a little sifted icing sugar. Serve cut into wedges. In the winter when there are no soft fruits available, sliced bananas and chopped preserved ginger make a nice filling.

Orange Cheesecake with Strawberries

1½ lb cream cheese
4 oz wheatmeal biscuits
1 oz butter
3 fl oz concentrated frozen
    orange juice (thawed)
2 oz castor sugar
The grated zest of
    ½ orange
½ lb strawberries
1 8-inch flan tin with a
    loose base.

First melt the butter, then crush the biscuits to fine crumbs using a rolling-pin. Then in a basin combine

9

them with the melted butter. Now press the biscuit mixture evenly over the base of the flan tin. Next grate the orange zest and blanch it in boiling water for five minutes (to get rid of the bitterness) then leave it to drain thoroughly.

In a large mixing bowl beat the cream cheese, sugar and concentrated orange juice until smooth and free from lumps, then beat in the orange rind. Pour the mixture into the flan tin, spreading it out evenly, cover with foil and chill thoroughly in the refrigerator for several hours. To serve, loosen the base from the side of the tin, and decorate the top of the cake with the strawberries.

Salads

However much of a champion of British cooking I may be, I have to admit that one thing we're particularly bad at in this country is salads. We *like* salads well enough, but we're not very imaginative when it comes to preparing them. There's a world of difference between a waterlogged lettuce doused with commercially made salad cream (that looks and tastes like metal polish) and a carefully prepared, crisp, fresh green salad glistening with a really good, flavoursome dressing. So Number One on my list is an ordinary Green Salad made with home-grown British lettuce – imported jet-set lettuces that have travelled thousands of miles to get here are *never* as good as our own.

Green Salad

If you can pick your own lettuce fresh from the garden, then you've really got the best possible. However, if you're not so lucky and you have to buy one, make sure it's fresh and doesn't look crushed and tired. Similarly when you get your lettuce home don't leave it waiting around too long.

Whatever kind of lettuce you buy the preparation is the same. First rule, don't cut the leaves with a knife – always tear the roots and leaves off with your hands (cutting with a knife tends to brown them round the edges). Always tear off the leaves whole as well, and only break them up just before dressing if you need to, because broken leaves tend to go limp much more quickly.

Commercially grown lettuces are never all that dusty, so try to avoid plunging them into bowls of water and dampening them unnecessarily. The delicate flavour of lettuce needs to be preserved at all costs, and flooding with water doesn't help. Instead take a damp piece of kitchen paper and simply wipe the leaves clean – it's less work in the long run because you haven't the bother of trying to get it dry again. If your lettuce is just too dirty for this, then plunge it very quickly into cold water and swing it round in a salad basket to get rid of the excess moisture, and hang in a cool dry place.

The next problem with lettuce, especially in very hot weather, is that it has a habit of going very limp. If this happens, just put it into a sealed polythene container in the lowest part of the refrigerator for about an hour or so, and this will recrisp the leaves – only don't overdo this, because refrigeration, however mild, does affect the flavour. None of the above operations will cause any bother – it's just a question of doing things the right way, instead of the wrong.

Dress the lettuce just before serving. Break up the leaves if they are too large, place them in a good-sized salad bowl and then coat the leaves with very little well-flavoured vinaigrette dressing (see page 19). Add some chopped parsley or watercress if you like, and it has been said that the only way to dress a salad is with your hands. I really agree with this, but if you're not too keen on the idea, you can use a spoon and fork instead. If the lettuce is dry the dressing will coat each leaf as you toss it round, and be very mean with the dressing because you don't want to end up with little pools at the bottom of the salad bowl. There – the nicest salad of all to accompany cold cuts, steaks and omelettes, even fish.

Tomato Salad

A tomato salad needs just as careful preparation and, properly made, it makes a good starter before a meal served with some crusty French bread and fresh butter. Choose firm but ripe tomatoes. Pour boiling water over them and in a minute or two the skins will slip off very easily.

Again, never prepare a tomato salad too far in advance, because once you slice tomatoes they go a bit woolly. Another important point is that you should use a large flat plate for them – or else smaller individual plates – because the slices shouldn't overlap each other, another thing that causes sogginess.

For my tomato salad I like to sprinkle on some very finely chopped raw onion and lots of fresh chopped parsley and perhaps a mere trace of sugar – and some fresh chopped basil leaves would be a luxurious addition, if your green fingers have been luckier than mine at rearing it. Once again, dress the salad at the last minute before serving.

Now, two salads that can be prepared in advance. First a delicious one made with early new potatoes. When you buy new potatoes, pick one up if you can and rub your thumb along it. If it's fresh the skin will just fall away under the pressure of your thumb and the potato itself will feel hard and firm.

New Potato Salad with Mint and Chives
(serves 4–6)

2 lb small new potatoes
2 sprigs mint
8 medium-sized spring onions, very finely chopped
3 tablespoons fresh chopped mint

2 tablespoons fresh chopped parsley
2 tablespoons fresh snipped chives
Vinaigrette dressing (see page 19)
Salt and freshly milled pepper

Wash the potatoes but *don't* scrape them (there's a lot of flavour in the delicate skins of new potatoes), place them in a saucepan with salt and a couple of sprigs of mint, then pour boiling water on them, enough to come about halfway up. Put on a tight-fitting lid and simmer them till tender, being very careful not to over-cook. About twenty to twenty-five minutes should be enough – test them with a skewer, they should be tender but firm. Over-cooking will make them watery and mushy.

Drain them in a collander then put them in a salad bowl. Chop them roughly with a knife, and then pour the dressing on while they're still warm. Mix thoroughly, and when the potatoes have cooled mix in the fresh herbs. Taste to check the seasoning and keep the salad in a cool place until needed.

Another really good salad that can be made in advance is a rice salad, which also happens to be very versatile inasmuch as it can incorporate what you have available – and this one incorporates practically everything.

Rice Salad
(serves 4)

1 teacup long-grain rice
2½ teacups boiling water
3 or 4 tablespoons vinaigrette dressing
3 spring onions, very finely chopped
2 inches cucumber, finely chopped
2 large tomatoes, skinned and finely chopped

½ red or green pepper, finely chopped
1 red dessert apple, chopped but not peeled
1 oz currants
1 oz walnuts, finely chopped
Salt and freshly milled pepper
Vinaigrette dressing (see page 19)

14

Place the rice and some salt in a saucepan, pour the boiling water over and bring it back to the boil, then stir once, put a lid on and simmer very gently for twenty-five minutes or so until all the liquid has been absorbed. Now empty the rice into a salad bowl, fluff it up with a fork and then pour the dressing over while it's still warm.

When it's cold, mix in all the other ingredients, adding a little more dressing if it needs it and tasting to check the seasoning. Keep in a cool place until needed.

Finally, my own favourite summer salad, Salad Niçoise, and to go with it a hot Herb and Garlic Loaf.

Salad Niçoise
(serves 4)

1 lettuce
$\frac{1}{4}$ lb cooked new potatoes, sliced
$\frac{1}{4}$ lb cooked french beans
$\frac{1}{2}$ small young cucumber, peeled and cut in smallish chunks
$\frac{3}{4}$ lb firm ripe tomatoes, skinned, de-seeded and quartered
2 oz black olives
2 hard-boiled eggs, peeled and quartered

1 8-oz tin tuna fish, well drained
1 tablespoon finely chopped onion, or spring onions
1 tablespoon fresh chopped parsley
1 2-oz tin anchovy fillets, well drained
Vinaigrette dressing with Garlic and Herbs, see page 19 (you won't need the full quantity of vinaigrette)

In a large salad bowl first arrange lettuce leaves around the base and sprinkle a little salad dressing. Then arrange the tomatoes and cucumbers in layers with a little more salad dressing, then add the onion, slices of potatoes and french beans. Now arrange the quartered hard-boiled eggs on top and the tuna fish, which should be broken up into chunky flakes. Finally decorate the salad with the strips of anchovy fillet, making a latticed effect (or whatever you like), then sprinkle on the black olives, the fresh chopped parsley and the rest of the dressing. Serve as soon as possible.

Salad Niçoise needs lots of crusty bread to accompany it or, even nicer, a hot herb and garlic loaf which is made as follows.

Hot Herb and Garlic Loaf

1 French stick loaf
3 oz butter (room temperature)
2 cloves garlic, crushed

2 tablespoons fresh chopped herbs (parsley and chives with a little tarragon and thyme if available)

Pre-heat the oven to gas mark 6 (400°F). First mix the butter, garlic and herbs together, then using a sharp knife make diagonal incisions along the loaf (as if you were slicing it – but not slicing right through). The loaf should stay joined at the base. Now spread each slice with butter on both sides (it's easiest to do this with your hands) and spread any remaining herb butter along the top and the sides of the loaf. Wrap the loaf in foil and bake it in the oven for about ten to fifteen minutes, and serve hot.

Salad Dressings

I can remember a time not all that long ago, fifteen years maybe, v hen British tourists would return from holidays abroad complaining bitterly about Continentals pouring oil on their food (and I'll bet our French cousins had a thing or two to say about our bottled salad cream too). Nowadays, however, proper salad dressings – the sort that enhance flavour rather than mask it – are becoming much more popular, and people are beginning to appreciate the enormous gulf between factory-made and homemade mayonnaise.

Before making a salad dressing such as vinaigrette or mayonnaise, there's one very important point to note. It's best to use olive oil, but olive oils vary so much that it's worth trying a few to find one you like – perhaps a strong, fruity oil tasting of olives (good for vinaigrette) or a milder oil that's more suitable for mayonnaise. This is very much a matter of personal taste of course, but once you find one you like it will work out cheaper if you buy it in bulk – a half-gallon drum will save quite a bit in the long run.

Homemade Mayonnaise

The whole process of making mayonnaise can seem quite frightening to beginners, and all those 'what to do if it curdles' paragraphs in cookery books can be very off-putting. However, I've studied the matter most carefully and observed absolute beginners making mayonnaise, and have come to the conclusion that perhaps, for the first few times, you do have to be careful about adding the oil, but as soon as you get the feel of it you'll find the whole operation laughably easy. My advice to beginners is to use a good groundnut oil the first few times, which isn't nearly so expensive and precious as olive oil.

To make about half a pint of mayonnaise (enough for

four people) you'll need a 1½-pint basin, a damp tea towel to hold it steady and an electric hand-mixer or balloon whisk. Into the basin put two large egg yolks together with one level teaspoon of mustard powder or Dijon mustard, one level teaspoon of salt and a few screws of freshly milled pepper. If you like, you can also add a small crushed clove of garlic, but it's not essential.

Have within arm's reach ½ pint of olive oil in a small jug and some white wine vinegar. Now start off by mixing the egg yolks thoroughly with the salt, mustard and pepper, then holding the jug of oil in one hand and the whisk in the other, add *one* drop of oil. Yes, I mean it – just one drop and when that's whisked in, another and another, making sure each drop is thoroughly whisked in. After several drops the mixture will begin to thicken, and then you can begin adding bigger drops. Once it has thickened you know you're past the danger point. When about half the oil is in, add a teaspoon of white wine vinegar, which will make it thinner. At this point you can start pouring in the oil in a thin steady stream, still whisking, until it's all in. Taste to check the seasoning, and add a drop more vinegar if it needs it. Store in a screw-top jar in a cool place (I've even kept mine on the very bottom shelf of the fridge for up to a week without any ill effects).

If the mayonnaise curdles – and this will happen if the oil is added too quickly at the beginning – instead of throwing the whole lot out, break another egg yolk into a clean bowl, and add the curdled mixture to that drop by drop.

(Note: If you prefer, you can use lemon juice instead of wine vinegar.)

If you don't like mayonnaise, or would like an occasional change, try this recipe from Eliza Acton's *Modern Cookery for Private Families* (modern, that was, in 1845).

English Salad Sauce

The yolks of 3 hard-
boiled eggs
$\frac{1}{4}$ pint double cream

4 teaspoons white wine
vinegar
2 pinches cayenne pepper
$\frac{1}{4}$ teaspoon salt

Bring the eggs to the boil in plenty of cold water (they must be completely covered) and give them eight minutes exactly from the time it starts boiling. Then run them under the cold tap to cool them – and stop them cooking any further. Peel away the shells and the whites, and place the yolks only in a mixing bowl.

Add a tablespoon of cold water and pound the yolks to a smooth paste with a wooden spoon. Add a couple of pinches of cayenne and the $\frac{1}{4}$ teaspoon of salt, then stir in the cream, bit by bit, mixing it smoothly as you go. When it's all in, add the vinegar and taste to check the seasoning. If you think your mixture's far too runny at this stage, fear not. Cover the bowl and leave it for a couple of hours in the refrigerator, after which time it will have thickened (it should have the consistency of thickish cream rather than mayonnaise).

Vinaigrette

Finally, a recipe for the famous Sauce Vinaigrette, or French Dressing as we sometimes call it. There are a million different versions and almost as many false rumours about how it should or should not be made. So here are a few points worth bearing in mind.

First of all, you need good ingredients, i.e. genuine wine vinegar – malt vinegar is far too strong and should *never* be allowed near a salad – and a good olive oil (unidentifiable cooking oils or corn oil are obviously not as good). Also, vinaigrette tastes so much better when freshly made, so don't make a huge bottle once a month. Make it as and when you need it – a few hours in advance is fine, but after being kept a day or two it loses its fresh flavour. Finally a quote from *Kettner's Book of the Table*, first published in 1877, which still holds good today when making a salad dressing: 'Be a counsellor with the salt, a miser with the vinegar and a spendthrift with the oil.'

1 tablespoon genuine wine vinegar (red or white)
1 teaspoon mustard (English or Dijon)
1 heaped teaspoon salt
Freshly milled black pepper
½ clove garlic crushed (only if you like it)
5 or 6 tablespoons olive oil

Put the above ingredients except the oil into a small screw-top jar and leave it for an hour or so for the salt to dissolve. Then add five or six tablespoons of olive oil, put the lid back on and shake the jar furiously to combine all the ingredients. Always shake the jar again before using the dressing.

Does a salad dressing need sugar? Personally I've never thought so. If you use the ratio of oil to vinegar that I've given the dressing won't be too sharp, and therefore won't need sugar to counteract the sharpness. But if you like a little sugar, then it's up to you. Lemon juice can be used instead of vinegar.

For a *Vinaigrette with Herbs* add a teaspoon each of fresh chopped parsley, chives and tarragon just before serving. Dried herbs are not really suitable for salad dressings, and they tend to look like small black specks that haven't been washed out of the lettuce.

Chicken Salad with Tarragon and Green Grapes
(serves 4)

1 cooked chicken (about 3 lb)
$\frac{1}{4}$ pint homemade mayonnaise (see above)
3 fl oz double cream
$\frac{1}{4}$ lb green grapes, peeled and de-pipped
1 tablespoon fresh chopped tarragon (if you can't get hold of fresh tarragon, use

1 heaped teaspoon of dried, soaked in warm water for five minutes then squeezed dry in kitchen paper)
2 or 3 spring onions
A few sprigs watercress
1 small lettuce
Salt and freshly milled pepper

Remove the skin from the chicken and slice the flesh into longish pieces where possible, then remove all the chicken from the bones and place all the meat in a bowl, seasoning with salt and pepper. In a separate bowl mix the mayonnaise thoroughly with the cream, adding the chopped tarragon and finely chopped spring onions. Now pour this sauce over the chicken, mix it well so that all the chicken pieces get a good coating, then arrange it on a plate of crisp lettuce leaves and garnish with green grapes and a few sprigs of watercress.

English Lamb

For flavour it would be hard to equal English lamb, especially around the months of June and July when our home-grown meat is in its prime season – and what's more there are delicious baby new potatoes, green peas and baby carrots to go with it as well as mint, rosemary and other fresh herbs. Someone once said that if you like the flavour of lamb, eat it with redcurrant jelly; and if you don't, eat it with mint sauce. I would agree if the mint sauce is made with *malt* vinegar, because it's lethal to flavour. My own favourite sauce (below) is made with both redcurrant jelly and mint, but if you're making an ordinary mint sauce, then use only the mildest of wine vinegars.

Lamb Baked with Butter and Herbs

1 shoulder or leg of lamb (weighing about 4 lb)	2 tablespoons fresh chopped parsley
3 oz butter (room temperature)	1 clove garlic, crushed
1 teaspoon crushed rosemary	Salt and freshly milled pepper
2 tablespoons fresh chopped mint	Cooking foil

Pre-heat the oven to gas mark 5 (375°F). Mix the butter, herbs and garlic together, adding a level teaspoon of salt and some freshly milled black pepper. Stab the joint in several places with a skewer, and then rub the herb butter all over the upper side (these stabs with the skewer will allow the butter to run into the joint during the cooking).

Now wrap the joint loosely in foil, sealing well. Place it in a meat roasting tin and cook it for two hours, then open out the foil and cook it for a further thirty minutes to brown nicely. With these cooking times the lamb will be slightly pink. If you like it well done give it a little extra time in the foil before opening it out. To serve, remove the joint to a warm serving dish and leave it in a warm place while you make the gravy.

Gravy

1 teaspoon plain flour   Vegetable stock
3 fl oz dry white wine   Seasoning

Empty the juices from the foil into the roasting tin, then tilt it slightly. You will see the meat juices and the fat separating, so spoon off most of the fat into a bowl and leave the juices in the tin. Now place the tin over a medium heat, and when it starts to bubble sprinkle in the flour and work it to a smooth paste using a wooden spoon, then cook it for a minute or so to brown. Now pour in the white wine and stock by degrees, stirring continuously and adding just enough stock to make a thin gravy. Taste to check the seasoning, pour into a jug and serve with the lamb.

If you are plain-roasting the lamb, this redcurrant, orange and mint jelly is a delicious accompaniment.

Redcurrant, Orange and Mint Jelly
(serves 6)

4 tablespoons authentic   The grated zest of
   redcurrant jelly (one   1 orange
   with a high fruit   1½ tablespoons fresh
   content)   chopped mint

Place the jelly in a small basin, break it up with a fork

then mix in the orange zest and the mint – and that's it. It must be the quickest sauce in the whole world, and it's absolutely delicious.

Mustard Glazed Lamb Chops or Cutlets
(serves 4)

8 lamb cutlets
2 tablespoons made-up mustard (English or Dijon)
3 tablespoons demarara sugar
Salt and freshly milled pepper

Pre-heat the grill to a high setting. Wipe the cutlets first with some absorbent kitchen paper to dry them, season them with salt and pepper, then spread both sides of each cutlet with mustard. Now dip them in the brown sugar, making sure they get an even coating, and grill them for a few minutes on each side, depending on their thickness. (These little cutlets are even nicer barbecued over charcoal.)

Fresh Salmon

Fresh Scotch salmon is undoubtedly the best in the world. Unfortunately during the early spring when it's at its best, few of us can afford to buy it, but in late June and July, however, prices will start to come down – and then it shouldn't cost more than good-quality steak. To cook salmon, you can forget about enormous fish kettles, coatings of aspic and the like. The very best way to cook it is slowly in the oven, wrapped in buttered foil. If it's going to be eaten cold it should be allowed to cool in the foil too, and have the skin removed only just before serving. This way it will keep deliciously moist and full of flavour. One thing you need, if you're going to buy salmon, is a reliable fishmonger. I know they are few and far between nowadays, but your salmon really does need to be in perfect condition.

Fresh Salmon
(serves 4)

1½ lb middle cut salmon (room temperature)
2 bayleaves
2 oz butter

Salt and freshly milled black pepper
1 large double piece of foil, well buttered

Pre-heat the oven to gas mark ½ (250°F). Wipe the salmon with some damp kitchen paper – don't wash it in water – then place it in the centre of a double sheet of foil. Put half the butter with the bayleaves in the centre cavity, and put the rest of the butter on top. Season with salt and pepper, then wrap the salmon up to make a parcel, folding the edges of the foil to seal the salmon inside. Place the parcel on a heatproof plate and bake it in the oven for one hour 10 minutes (when cooked, the salmon skin will come away very easily). If the salmon is to be served cold, allow it to cool <u>without</u> unwrapping the foil. Try if possible to cook it on the same day and leave it in a cool place – though it's best not to put it into the refrigerator.

If you have a large piece of salmon, cook in exactly the same way, giving a 2-lb piece $1\frac{1}{2}$ hours, 3-lb $2\frac{1}{4}$ hours, 4-lb $2\frac{1}{2}$ hours, and 5-lb $2\frac{3}{4}$ hours. Likewise, for salmon trout use exactly the same method and cooking times according to weight. Salmon steaks cooked in this way need twenty to twenty-five minutes for steaks weighing up to 8 oz each.

Finally, for a party a whole salmon will serve a lot of people without a great deal of fuss. A whole 8-lb salmon will easily serve sixteen people and you cook it exactly as above but severing it in half first (unless you have an extremely large oven), making two foil parcels, cooking them for $2\frac{1}{2}$ hours and before serving placing the two halves together again and covering the join with slices of cucumber, lemon and bunches of watercress.

There are many excellent sauces that can be served with cold salmon – probably the most usual accompaniment would be mayonnaise (see page 17). However, for a change, here are two very simply prepared sauces that go particularly well with cold salmon and salmon trout.

Avocado Sauce
(serves 4)

1 small or $\frac{1}{2}$ fairly large avocado pear

A 5-oz carton soured cream

1 tablespoon fresh lemon juice

$\frac{1}{2}$ clove garlic, crushed to a pulp

Salt and freshly milled black pepper

Scrape the avocado flesh away from the skin into a

bowl, making sure you scrape away the very green bit next to the skin as this is important for the colour of the sauce. Then mash it to a purée together with the lemon juice and garlic, and combine it with the soured cream, mixing thoroughly until you have a smooth, pale green, creamy sauce. Cover the basin tightly with cellophane wrap to stop the avocado discolouring and chill in the refrigerator till needed. Do make this sauce the same day as it's required, since it does tend to discolour if left too long.

Cucumber and Soured Cream Sauce
(serves 4)

4 inches peeled cucumber
A 5-oz carton soured
　cream
1 tablespoon chopped
　tarragon (or if
tarragon is unavailable,
use 1 teaspoon chopped
mint)
Salt and freshly milled
　black pepper

Slice the cucumber thinly, then cut the slices in half and mix thoroughly with the rest of the ingredients.

Salmon Coulibiac

(serves 4)

1 13½-oz packet puff
  pastry
8–10 oz cooked salmon,
  flaked
3 oz butter
3 oz long-grain rice
8 fl oz stock
1 medium onion, finely
  chopped
4 oz button mushrooms,
  thinly sliced

½ teaspoon dried dill weed
1 dessertspoon lemon
  juice
2 hard-boiled eggs,
  roughly chopped
1 tablespoon fresh
  chopped parsley
Beaten eggs
Salt and freshly milled
  black pepper

Pre-heat the oven to gas mark 6 (400°F). Melt 1 oz of butter in a saucepan, then stir in the rice, and when it's all got a good coating of butter pour in approximately 8 fl oz of stock. Stir once and when it reaches simmering point, put on a lid and allow it to cook gently till all the water has been absorbed – about twelve to fifteen minutes. Then take the pan off the heat, stir in the cooked salmon and parsley and let the rice cool.

Meanwhile melt the rest of the butter in a frying-pan and soften the onion in it for ten minutes, then add the mushroom and dill and lemon juice, and cook for a further five minutes. Now remove the pan from the heat, stir in the chopped hard-boiled eggs, and season with salt and freshly milled black pepper. Allow the mixture to cool.

Roll out the pastry to approximately fourteen inches square then cut it into two rectangles, one 6½ inches wide, the other 7½ inches wide. Now lay the larger one on a lightly greased baking sheet, then arrange half the salmon and rice mixture down the centre, being careful to leave a one-inch border all round. Spoon the mushroom mixture on top, then cover with the rest of the salmon and press and pat the mixture into a neat shape. Brush the border of the pastry with beaten egg, then place the other half on top, sealing well all round.

Next, brush the surface with beaten egg, then roll the sealed edges over and press again – this time with a fork. Finally make six diagonal cuts in the top of the coulibiac, bake in the oven for thirty minutes. Serve with a jug of melted butter or some soured cream, whichever you prefer.

Summer Soups

I can think of nothing nicer on a warm summer's evening than to start a meal with some refreshing icy-cold soup – especially at the height of the English salad season when so many home-grown ingredients are available. What you have to remember, though, is that if you're going to serve a cold soup, it's got to be very cold and thoroughly chilled. There's nothing worse than trying to guess whether a soup is a hot one that's gone cold or a cold one turned hot. If it's a very warm day I often find it helps to chill the soup bowls too for an hour or so before serving.

My first soup, Gazpacho – or Salad Soup as I often call it – is probably the most famous of all. In Spain there are 101 versions of it, varying from region to region. And if, as they do, you serve the various bowls of 'bits and pieces' to go with it and lots of crusty fresh bread, it's a meal in itself.

Gazpacho
(serves 6)

1½ lb firm ripe tomatoes
A 4-inch piece of cucumber, peeled and chopped
2 or 3 spring onions, peeled and chopped
½ large red or green pepper, chopped
2 cloves garlic, crushed
4 tablespoons olive oil

1½ tablespoons wine vinegar
1 heaped teaspoon fresh chopped basil, marjoram or thyme (depending on what's available)
½ pint cold water
4 ice cubes
Salt and freshly milled black pepper

Begin by placing the tomatoes in a bowl and pouring boiling water over them to loosen the skins, which after a minute or two will slip off very easily. Halve the tomatoes, scoop out and discard the seeds, and roughly chop the flesh. Now place the tomatoes, cucumber, spring onion and chopped pepper in a liquidiser, adding a seasoning of salt and pepper, the herbs, oil and wine vinegar. Then blend everything at top speed until the soup is absolutely smooth. Combine all the ingredients first, if your liquidiser is very small, then blend in two or three batches. Taste to check the seasoning and pour the soup into a bowl. Add a little cold water to thin it slightly (anything from $\frac{1}{4}$ to $\frac{1}{2}$ pint), then cover the bowl with foil and chill thoroughly. Serve the soup with four ice cubes floating in it and a garnish handed round separately.

For the garnish

$\frac{1}{2}$ large red or green pepper, very finely chopped

4 inches peeled cucumber, finely chopped

2 spring onions, finely chopped

1 hard-boiled egg, finely chopped

1 heaped tablespoon fresh chopped parsley

Combine all these ingredients together with a seasoning of salt and freshly milled black pepper, and hand them round at the table together with small croûtons of bread fried till crisp in olive oil, well drained and cooled.

Chilled Cucumber Soup
(serves 4–6)

This deliciously light and subtle soup is incredibly easy and quick to make. However it *does* need fresh British cucumbers, and not the tasteless imported ones.

2 medium-sized firm
  young cucumbers
½ pint natural yoghurt
¼ pint soured cream
A little milk
1 clove garlic, crushed
1 dessertspoon fresh
  lemon juice

1 heaped teaspoon fresh
  chopped mint
A few slices lemon, cut
  very thinly
Salt and freshly milled
  pepper

First of all peel the cucumbers and slice them. Reserve a few slices to garnish the soup, then place the rest in a liquidiser along with the yoghurt, soured cream and crushed garlic. Switch on and blend at the highest speed till smooth. Add a seasoning of salt and pepper and lemon juice, then pour the soup into a tureen and if it seems to be a little too thick, thin it with some cold milk. Now stir in the fresh chopped mint, cover with foil or with a lid and chill thoroughly for several hours before serving. To serve ladle the soup into individual soup bowls and float a few thin slices of cucumber and a thin slice of lemon on each one.

Homemade Tomato Soup
(serves 3 or 4)

I make no apologies for including a recipe for real homemade tomato soup. Tinned, it's uniform and dull – homemade, it's the freshest, most fragrant summer soup you can think of, and it's equally nice hot or cold.

1½ lb firm ripe tomatoes	½ pint stock
1 medium onion, chopped small	Some fresh chopped basil
	½ teaspoon sugar
1 medium potato, chopped small	Olive oil
1 clove garlic	Salt and freshly milled pepper

Gently heat up just over one tablespoon of olive oil in a thick-based saucepan, then put the onion, potato and a few fresh chopped basil leaves (or if they're unavailable, parsley) in to melt slowly without browning – about ten to fifteen minutes. Meanwhile put your tomatoes into a large bowl, pour boiling water over, then in a minute or two slip their skins off. Chop the flesh of the tomatoes roughly then add them to the potato and onion, stirring round with a wooden spoon. Next stir in the stock (mixed, if you like, with a teaspoonful of tomato purée), season with salt and pepper, add ½ teaspoon of sugar, then on with the lid and let it all simmer gently for around twenty-five minutes. When the soup's ready, pass the whole lot through a sieve to extract the pips. Taste to check the seasoning, cover and chill thoroughly if it is to be served cold. Otherwise serve immediately.

Summer Entertaining (1)

In one way, entertaining in the summer months can become fraught with indecision, because there's always so *much* to choose from. Still, it's a pleasant dilemma. In this programme we're going to tackle the first and last courses.

To start with I've chosen Poached Trout with Herbs, and to finish off the meal (which includes Duck as a main course, see page 37), a revival of the much-neglected English fruit fool. There's a choice of rhubarb or green gooseberry, either of which makes a perfect ending to a summer's meal.

Poached Trout with Herbs
(serves 4)

4 trout (weighing approximately 6 oz each)	1 sprig fresh thyme (or 1 teaspoon dried thyme)
Salt	3 tablespoons fresh parsley, finely chopped
6 whole peppercorns	
4 bay leaves	2 tablespoons fresh snipped chives
1 small onion (peeled and cut into rings)	4 fl oz dry white wine
1 lemon	3 oz butter

Place the trout either in a large frying pan or a thick-based roasting tin. Now sprinkle over them a little salt and throw in the peppercorns. Next add the bay leaves, one in between each trout. Lay onion rings over the top, cut half the lemon into slices and arrange them here and there. Add the thyme and sprinkle one tablespoon of chopped parsley over everything. Finally add the wine and enough cold water just to cover the fish. Bring it to the boil on top of the stove and let it simmer gently, uncovered, for six minutes if the trout are fresh or

Pears in Sweet Spiced Coffee

Poaching Liquid := 1.5 Litres coffee
525g soft dark sugar
the pared zest & juice of 2 large
oranges,
3 tbsp. roughly chopped preserved ginger
1.5 cm cinnamon stick
8 pears, firm, ripe pears
peeled + cored.

Sauce:
250 ml poaching liquid
+ tsp. cornflour
2 tbsp fresh orange juice

Garnish = orange segments
_____
+ Mint sprigs

Combine all poaching ingredients
Simmer for 4 mins on low heat. Add Pears
+ continue to simmer gently until cooked.
Leave in liquid (Pears) while ready. Soak

Pour 250 ml of poaching liquid into Sauce Pan
dissolve orange juice in orange juice add to
liquid. Simmer for 3 mins. Set aside to cool.
Serve with ice cream & cinnamon sticks.

twenty minutes if they are frozen. In a small basin mix the remaining parsley and chives with the butter and then divide the mixture into four portions. When the trout are ready, carefully lift them out with a fish slice allowing each one to drain for a few seconds and serve with the parsley butter and the other half of the lemon cut into wedges.

Rhubarb Fool
(serves 4)

1 lb rhubarb	1 heaped teaspoon
3 oz demarara sugar	ground ginger
	8 fl oz double cream

Pre-heat the oven to gas mark 4 (350°F). Cut the rhubarb into one-inch chunks, place it in an ovenproof baking dish and sprinkle on the sugar and ginger. Place it in the oven (without a cover) for twenty-five minutes or until the rhubarb is tender but still holds its shape. Now either liquidise or press it through a nylon sieve. Taste while it's still hot, and add a little more sugar or ginger if you think it needs it. As soon as the purée is quite cold, whip the cream to thicken very slightly (but not *too* much) and then mix it with the rhubarb. Pour the fool into tall glasses or little custard cups. Cover them with foil and chill in the refrigerator.

Gooseberry Fool
(serves 4)

1 lb hard green	4 oz castor sugar
gooseberries	8 fl oz double cream

Prepare in exactly the same way as for the Rhubarb Fool (omitting the ginger), and if you're going to sieve the fruit instead of liquidising it, there's no need to top and tail the gooseberries.

Serve the fruit fools with little langue de chat biscuits (obtainable at delicatessens and specialised food shops).

Summer Entertaining (2)

Duck has always been a favourite entertaining item for me, simply because it will sit in the oven, needing little or no attention at all, until you're ready for it. And if guests do happen to be late, or take longer than usual over the first course, a duck will put up with that without spoiling.

My own method of cooking duck is a little unorthodox in that I like the skin to be really crisp, and so I cook it for quite a long time. It's a little less meaty this way, but far less fatty – and much nicer for it to my mind.

Duck with Cherries
(serves 4)

1 large fresh duck (weighing around 6 lb)	1 bunch watercress
$\frac{1}{4}$ pint red wine	Salt and freshly milled black pepper
$\frac{1}{4}$ lb Morello cherry jam	

Pre-heat the oven to gas mark 7 (425°F). Place the duck in a roasting tin, prick the fleshy parts with a skewer, sprinkle it with salt and pepper and place it in the oven just as it is – don't add fat or anything. After twenty minutes turn the oven down to gas mark 4 (350°F) and cook the duck for three hours. During the cooking time take it out of the oven a couple of times and drain off the fat from the corner of the tin into a bowl (this fat is very good for frying or roasting potatoes).

During the last ten minutes of the cooking time, turn the heat up again to gas mark 7 (425°F) for a final crisp. Remove the duck from the roasting tin on to a board and, using your sharpest carving knife, simply cut it into four, across and then lengthways. A pair of kitchen scissors is sometimes useful for this operation. Arrange the quarters on a warmed serving dish, pour the sauce over and garnish with sprigs of watercress. Morello cherry sauce is made as follows.

Morello Cherry Sauce

In a small saucepan bring the wine to simmering point, reduce slightly, then add the jam. Stir well with a wooden spoon and simmer for a further five minutes. This sauce can be made well in advance, and then reheated when needed. (Note: the jam for this sauce must be *Morello* cherry – and say so on the label. It is normally obtainable at delicatessens and specialised food shops.)

Braised Peas with Lettuce and Spring Onion
(serves 4)

2 lb young peas, freshly shelled	8 spring onions
6 lettuce leaves	2 oz butter
	A pinch sugar and salt

Trim the onions – you only need the bulbous white part – and break the lettuce leaves into wide strips. Then melt the butter in a thick-based saucepan, add the onions, lettuce and peas. Stir well, then add four tablespoons of water, a pinch of sugar and a level teaspoon of salt. Bring to simmering point, then cover the saucepan and let it cook over a very, very gentle heat for about twenty to twenty-five minutes (keeping an eye on it, and shaking the pan now and then to prevent the vegetables sticking). Add just a little more water if you think it needs it.

Picnic Food

I think the best picnics are the simplest. Secretly we may all dream of elegant Edwardian picnics, complete with chauffeur and butler, with salmon, strawberries and a bottle or two of champagne cooling in some crystal-clear stream. But the fact is that, even with the most sophisticated equipment, the more elaborate the food, the worse it travels; and what the practical, modern-day picnic needs is food that's easily transportable. I believe picnic food should be bold, and full of flavour. Rough, peasant-type food always tastes good in the open air – even rough, peasant-type wines seem to mellow in the warm sunshine.

First, then, a meat loaf which can be taken on a picnic whole, then cut in thick slices to serve.

Meat Loaf

1 lb lean minced beef (from a reliable butcher)
½ lb minced pork (or pork sausage-meat)
2 medium onions, minced
1 small green pepper, finely chopped
1 dessertspoon tomato purée
1 fat clove garlic, crushed

1 level teaspoon dried mixed herbs
2 tablespoons fresh chopped parsley
2 slices white bread from a large loaf
3 tablespoons milk
1 egg, beaten
Salt and freshly milled black pepper
A 2-lb loaf tin

Pre-heat the oven to gas mark 5 (375°F). Put the minced beef in a large mixing bowl with the pork, onion, chopped pepper, tomato purée and garlic and give everything a thorough mixing, seasoning well with salt and freshly milled pepper. Cut the crusts off the bread, soak it in the milk, then squeeze the excess milk out of it and add it to the rest of the ingredients, along with the mixed herbs and the parsley. Now give the mixture another thorough mixing, and finally stir in the beaten egg to bind it all together.

Press the mixture into a 2-lb loaf tin, spreading evenly, then bake it in the oven for 1¼ hours. When it's cooked it will have shrunk and begun to come away from the sides of the tin. Allow it to cool in the tin, wrap it in a double sheet of foil and take it to the picnic wrapped in a cloth or in an oblong plastic box. (Note: Meat loaf is delicious served cold with pickles and salad. It also goes very well sliced and put into sandwiches or rolls, and for a main meal at home serve it hot with a homemade tomato and chilli sauce, see page 56).

Banana and Walnut Cake
(serves 4–6)

1½ oz butter, and	8 oz plain flour
1½ oz lard (both at room temperature)	2 level teaspoons baking powder
4 oz castor sugar	4 medium-sized bananas
1 egg, beaten	2 oz shelled walnuts, coarsely chopped
The grated zest of 1 lemon	A 2-lb loaf tin, buttered
The grated zest of 1 orange	

Pre-heat the oven to gas mark 4 (350°F). In a mixing bowl cream the fats together then add the sugar, and beat until the mixture becomes a pale, fluffy cream that drops off the spoon easily. Now beat in the beaten egg, a teaspoonful at a time, beating the mixture well after each addition. Next mix in the grated orange and lemon zest. Sift the flour and baking powder together then,

40

using a metal spoon, fold the flour carefully into the mixture.

Now peel the bananas and in a basin mash them to a creamy pulp with a large fork, then mix them into the cake mixture together with the chopped walnuts. Spoon the mixture into the prepared tin, level it off with the back of a tablespoon, and bake it in the centre of the oven for fifty to sixty minutes, or until a skewer inserted into the centre comes out clean and there are no sizzling noises. Cool on a wire cooling tray. Serve cut into thick slices, spread with butter.

Quiches and Tarts

In England it's a tart, in France it's a quiche and there are very many different versions on both sides of the Channel. I suppose the most famous French version is the classic Quiche Lorraine from Alsace-Lorraine, a delicious combination of bacon, thick cream and eggs. Of course, there are any number of truly 'authentic' varieties, and in Paris a Quiche Lorraine will nearly always contain thin slivers of Gruyère cheese.

Just as famous in its way is the old-fashioned English custard tart, light and creamy with a lovely brown-speckled nutmeg surface. But whether it's savoury or sweet, the tart is one of the most versatile of dishes, with unlimited variations and ingredients that are nearly always to hand.

There are a number of hard and fast rules attached to successful tart-making, the most important being that *tins* should always be used for baking, because metal is a much better conductor of heat than pyrex, earthenware or porcelain, and the pastry will cook much better and more evenly in tins. The second point is that, when you pre-heat the oven in the normal way you should pre-heat a baking sheet at the same time. This will ensure that the underneath pastry will cook crisply and not turn soggy.

Cream, Bacon and Onion Tart
(serves 4)

4 oz plain flour, sifted
A pinch salt
1 oz butter or margarine

1 oz pure lard
Cold water

For the filling

6 rashers streaky bacon,
    chopped
1 small onion, chopped
$\frac{1}{2}$ pint double cream
2 large eggs

Butter
Salt and freshly milled
    black pepper
1 greased 8-inch flan tin

Pre-heat the oven (with a baking sheet) to gas mark 4 (350°F). First quickly make up the pastry then roll it out fairly thinly and line the flan tin with it, pressing it down firmly all round the edge, and pricking the base all over with a fork. Pre-bake the pastry case for 15 minutes, then take it out of the oven and increase the heat to gas mark 5, 375°F. For the filling, gently soften the onion in butter for five minutes or so then add the chopped bacon and cook that for a further five minutes until the fat starts to run. Whisk the eggs thoroughly now, then whisk the cream into them and season with freshly milled pepper, but not too much salt (because there will be some in the bacon).

Now, using a draining spoon, transfer the bacon and onion to the tart, arranging it evenly over the base. Then pour in the egg and cream mixture, place the tart on the baking sheet in the oven, and bake it for about thirty-five to forty minutes or until the centre feels set and the filling is golden brown and puffy. I think this is nicest served straight out of the oven, but it can be made in advance and warmed in the oven again, or it's still extremely nice eaten cold. And to be more economical it could be made with half cream and half milk, or even all milk, instead of cream.

There are very many alternative fillings that can be used with the recipe above:

Cheese and Onion Tart using 2 oz grated Cheddar cheese
    and one medium onion

Leek and Bacon Tart using $\frac{1}{2}$ lb leeks and three rashers bacon

Asparagus and Cheese Tart using $\frac{3}{4}$ lb asparagus and $1\frac{1}{2}$ oz grated Gruyère cheese

Salmon Tart using $\frac{1}{2}$ lb cooked salmon with grated nutmeg

Kipper Tart using $\frac{1}{2}$ lb grilled kipper fillets

English Custard Tart
(serves 4–6)

Use the ingredients for the pastry as above, and for the filling:

$\frac{1}{2}$ pint double cream
3 large fresh eggs
1 tablespoon castor
   sugar

Freshly grated whole
   nutmeg

Pre-heat the oven to gas mark 4 (350°F). Make the pastry and line the flan tin and pre-cook as in the previous recipe. Break the eggs into a bowl, then take a pastry brush and brush a little of the egg *white* over the base of the pastry – which will help stop the pastry rising during the cooking and coming to the top. Now whisk the eggs thoroughly, and then whisk in the sugar and cream.

Pour the mixture into the flan case, cover the surface with freshly grated nutmeg, place the tart in the oven on a baking sheet, and bake for thirty to forty minutes or until the centre feels set. Serve either warm or chilled. (Note: The reason the pastry in the custard tart sometimes rises to the top is often because the oven heat is too high. If you think your oven is hotter than it should be, keep the tart on a low shelf.)

Egg Dishes

Eggs, in spite of today's high prices, are still an economical source of protein and one thing we can thank the Common Market for is the EEC ruling that all egg-boxes must be date-stamped. After years of desperately trying to find a reliable supply of really fresh eggs, we can now know just how long they've been sitting on the shelf before we buy them. An egg's freshness is supposed to deteriorate after about three weeks, so always buy your eggs (with a recent date-stamp of course) as and when you need them.

No programme on eggs would be complete without some sort of omelette and this one, from France, will provide a delicious meal for two people in a matter of minutes.

Omelette Savoyarde
(serves 2)

4 large eggs
1 large onion, chopped
3 rashers bacon, chopped roughly but not too small
2 medium-sized cooked potatoes, chopped

2 oz Gruyère cheese, cut into thin slivers
A little butter and oil
Salt and freshly milled black pepper

Begin by melting a little butter and oil in a medium-sized frying-pan, then gently cook the onions and bacon in it for ten minutes. Next add the chopped potatoes and let them colour a little for five minutes or so, stirring them round the pan. At this point switch on your grill to high.

Arrange the slivers of Gruyère cheese over the other ingredients in the pan, beat the eggs with a fork (not too much) and season them with pepper and just a little salt.

Turn the heat under the frying pan up to its highest and pour the eggs in. Using a palette knife, draw the outside of the omelette in, allowing the liquid egg to escape round the edges. Then place the pan under the hot grill for the top to set. Serve the omelette flat, cut in wedges – do not attempt to fold it.

Florentine Eggs
(serves 2)

1 lb fresh spinach	2 tablespoons double
4 large fresh eggs	cream
1 oz flour	1 tablespoon grated
$1\frac{1}{2}$ oz butter	Parmesan cheese
$\frac{1}{2}$ pint milk	Nutmeg
3 oz grated Cheddar	A little extra butter
cheese	Salt and freshly/milled
	black pepper

Pre-heat the oven to gas mark 4 (350°F). Prepare the spinach by washing it in several changes of cold water, tear out any tough stalky bits, and pack the spinach into a saucepan with some salt – no need to add any water, just place the saucepan over a medium heat, put a lid on, and let it cook for about ten minutes or so, stirring it round a couple of times during the cooking.

While that's cooking prepare the sauce by melting the butter in a saucepan, then stir in the flour and cook it for a minute or two. Now gradually add the milk bit by bit, stirring well after each addition until you have a smooth sauce. Add the cheese, season to taste with a little salt and freshly milled pepper, and let it cook over a very gentle heat for about five minutes.

Meanwhile drain the spinach in a collander, pressing it with a plate to squeeze all the water out, then arrange the spinach in a buttered gratin dish, grate a little nut-meg over it and sprinkle on one tablespoon of cream. Now make four depressions in the spinach using the back of a tablespoon, carefully break the eggs into each depression, season with salt and pepper.

Stir the extra tablespoon of cream into the cheese sauce, and pour it all over the eggs. Sprinkle with parmesan cheese and bake in the centre of the oven for 20–25 minutes, by which time the eggs will be just set and the cheese sauce nice and bubbly.

Piperade
(serves 2)

This is a dish from the Basque region of France, where they serve it with a thick slice of Bayonne ham. But even on its own it makes a substantial supper dish for two people.

2 green peppers, deseeded and cut into strips
1 lb tomatoes, skinned, deseeded and chopped
2 medium onions, chopped small
1 or 2 cloves garlic, crushed (how much is up to you)
$\frac{1}{2}$ teaspoon dried basil
4 large fresh eggs
Butter and olive oil
Salt and freshly milled black pepper

Melt a knob of butter and a dessertspoon of olive oil in a shallow heavy pan and add the onions, cooking them very gently for ten minutes without browning. Now add the crushed garlic, tomatoes and peppers, stir every-thing around a little, season with salt and pepper and basil, and cook without covering for another twenty

47

minutes or so (the peppers should be slightly under-done).

Now beat the eggs thoroughly, pour them into the pan and, using a wooden spoon, stir just as you would for scrambled eggs. When the mixture starts to thicken and the eggs are almost cooked, remove the pan from the heat, continuing to stir, and serve immediately (as with scrambled eggs, do be very careful not to over-cook).

Spare Parts Cooking

I hate the word offal – the very sound of it is guaranteed to put apprehensive offal-eaters right off. Hence spare parts. However, nutritionists insist that all of us would do well to eat liver or kidneys at least once a week, because they are so rich in essential vitamins. Equally important, I think, is the fact that they are so economical, partly because you need less per person than with ordinary meat. And unlike other cheaper cuts of meat, these cook quickly, making them ideal for speedy family meals.

Kidneys in Fresh Tomato Sauce
(serves 2, or double for 4)

6 lamb's kidneys
$\frac{3}{4}$ lb ripe red tomatoes
1 medium onion,
   chopped
1 clove garlic, crushed
$\frac{3}{4}$ teaspoon dried basil

1 level tablespoon
   tomato purée
1 level dessertspoon flour
Olive oil
Salt and freshly milled
   black pepper

Prepare the kidneys by peeling off the skins, cutting them in half and snipping out the white cores with some scissors (it's most important to take out the cores – if you don't the kidneys will be tough). In a medium-sized saucepan cook the onions and garlic gently in some olive oil for six minutes or so. Meanwhile pour boiling water over the tomatoes, slip the skins off, discard most of the seeds, and chop the flesh up roughly. Now add the kidneys to the onion, turn the heat up a little and let the kidneys brown, stirring them and turning them around. Next sprinkle in the flour and cook it for a minute or two, then add the chopped tomatoes, tomato purée and basil. Have another good stir, season with salt and pepper, cover the saucepan and let it simmer over a gentle heat for about twenty minutes. Serve with rice.

Liver in Soured Cream Sauce
(serves 4)

1 lb lamb's liver (ask the butcher to cut it into thin slices)
1 medium onion
½ lb mushrooms

A 5-oz carton soured cream
2½ oz butter
Freshly grated nutmeg
Salt and freshly milled black pepper

Peel the onion, then slice it into very thin rings. Now slice the rings in half and separate them, so that you have thin slivers of onion in little half-moon shapes. Melt 2 oz of butter in a large thick-based frying-pan, and gently soften the onion in it for ten minutes. While they're softening, wipe the mushrooms, take the stalks off, then slice the stalks and the caps thinly and add them to the onions (stirring them around) and cook them for a further five minutes.

Prepare the liver by slicing it into the thinnest strips possible, each strip being about 1½ inches long. Turn the heat up a bit under the pan, add the liver then brown it quickly, moving it around and turning the pieces over. Then turn the heat down and stir in the soured cream. Season with salt and freshly milled pepper and some grated nutmeg, and let it all simmer very gently for five minutes. Just before serving, stir in a small lump of butter. Serve immediately with plain rice and a green salad.

Kidneys in Jacket Potatoes
(serves 4)

4 large potatoes	2 oz butter
4 lamb's kidneys, skinned and cored	Oil
8 rashers streaky bacon	Salt and freshly milled pepper
A little made-up English or Dijon mustard	

Pre-heat the oven to gas mark 5 (375°F). Clean the potatoes by wiping them with a damp cloth – or if they're very dirty, by scrubbing them. Then dry them as well as possible (if you wash them early, you can leave them to dry for an hour or two). Rub the lightest film of oil into the skins of the potatoes (this makes them crisp), then bake them in the oven for 1 to 1½ hours, depending on their size. Test to see if they're cooked with a skewer.

When the potatoes are cooked, remove them from the oven and turn the heat up to gas mark 6 (400°F). Then holding them in a cloth (they're very hot!) make an incision with a knife lengthways and crossways, and lift the four corners up and pull them back a bit. Now make a depression in the centre of each potato, using a table-spoon. Season well with salt and pepper, and add a knob of butter to each one. Then spread the rashers of bacon with mustard and wrap two round each kidney, lay one in each potato and return them to the oven for thirty minutes. Serve immediately with a green salad on the side.

Pâtés

It can't be denied that the French make the best pâtés and terrines in the world. In Britain we seem to have lost the art of potting meat, fish and game, and few of our traditional raised pies (pâtés en croûte) get made nowadays. So it is to France that we look for inspiration, and both the pâtés in the programme are adapted from French country recipes.

It's always so useful to have some pâté in the house. They will keep for up to a week, stored in the lowest part of the refrigerator, and they are ideal standbys for a busy weekend. You can serve one for a light lunch with crusty bread and salad, for a first course at an evening meal, or for a late snack with hot toast.

Country Pâté

1 lb lean minced beef
1 lb fat belly pork, minced
½ lb pig's liver, minced
4 fl oz dry white wine
1 fl oz brandy
2 cloves garlic, crushed
6 black peppercorns

6 juniper berries
6 oz fat streaky bacon, chopped
1 level teaspoon salt
¼ teaspoon ground mace
A 2-lb loaf-tin or terrine

Buy the meats from a reliable butcher and, if you give him plenty of notice, he'll probably mince them for you. To make the pâté, place the meats in a large bowl with the chopped bacon and mix them all very thoroughly Add the salt and mace, then crush the peppercorns on a flat surface using the back of a tablespoon, do the same with the juniper berries, then add both the crushed pepper and juniper to the meat.

Now pour both the wine and the brandy over, have another really good mix, then cover the bowl with a cloth and leave it in a cool place for a couple of hours. To cook the pâté, pack the mixture into a loaf-tin, then place it in a meat roasting tin half-filled with hot water, and bake for about 1½ hours. By the time it's cooked the pâté will have shrunk quite a bit. Remove it from the oven, and allow it to cool without draining any of the juices (because, when cold, the surrounding fat will keep the pâté moist).

When the pâté is cold, place a double strip of foil along the top and put a few weights on to press it down for a few hours – this pressing isn't essential, it just helps to make the pâté less crumbly when you cut it. Serve the pâté with hot toast, crusty bread or, even better, with croûtons of bread baked till crisp in the oven.

Rillettes de Tours (Pork Pâté)
(serves 4)

2 lb piece belly pork (ask the butcher to remove the rind and bones for you)
½ lb back pork fat
4 fl oz dry white wine
¼ teaspoon powdered mace
6 black peppercorns
6 juniper berries
2 cloves garlic
1 dessertspoon fresh thyme
Salt
2-pint earthenware terrine

Pre-heat the oven to gas mark 1 (275°F). Take your sharpest knife and cut the pork lengthways into long strips about one inch wide, then cut each strip across and across again into smaller strips, and place these in an earthenware terrine. Cut the fat into small pieces too, and mix these in – the excess amount of fat will help to keep the pork properly moist during the cooking. Now add the thyme, along with the peppercorns and juniper berries (both crushed with the back of a tablespoon) and about a heaped teaspoon of salt, then pour in the wine.

Mix everything around to distribute the flavours, cover the terrine, place it in the centre of the oven and leave it there for four hours. After that, taste a piece of pork and add more salt and pepper if necessary. Now empty everything into a large sieve standing over a bowl, and let all the fat drip through (press the meat gently to extract the fat).

Take a couple of forks next, and pull the meat into shreds (sometimes it is pounded instead, but personally I think it's worth persevering with the fork method). Then pack the rillettes lightly into an earthenware terrine – not pressing down too hard – pour a little of the strained fat over and keep in a cool place until needed.

Summer Extras

The hardest thing of all, when you're planning a television series, is choosing just which recipes to include. The producer of Family Fare, Betty White, and myself have spent hours of swopping, rearranging and making short-lists to reach the final selection. Inevitably, there were many lovely recipes which had to be dropped.

Luckily, however, there were a few pages to spare in this booklet, so we have taken full advantage of this to include here a few of the close-runners that we didn't have time for in the actual programmes. I'm sure you will enjoy them as much as the others.

Old English Summer Soup
(serves 4)

1 small cabbage lettuce, washed and shredded	3 oz butter
6 spring onions, finely chopped	1½ pints chicken stock
2 medium-sized potatoes, finely diced	1 bunch fresh-snipped chives
½ cucumber, chopped	Salt and freshly milled black pepper

Start by melting the butter in a saucepan, then stir in the potato, spring onions, lettuce and cucumber. Stir it all round in the butter then, keeping the heat very low, cover the saucepan and let everything sweat for 10 minutes. Now pour in the stock, stir again and season with salt and pepper. Put the lid on and let it simmer gently for another 20 minutes.

Now you can either press the whole lot through a sieve or whiz to a purée in a liquidiser. Taste to check the seasoning, reheat and serve with the chives stirred in at the last moment. Alternatively you can serve this soup chilled – it's just as delicious.

Tomato and Chilli Sauce
(serves 2 or 3)

¾ lb red ripe tomatoes,
peeled, de-seeded and
  chopped
1 small onion, finely
  chopped
1 clove garlic, crushed
1 teaspoon tomato
  purée

1 dessertspoon fresh
  chopped basil
¼ teaspoon chilli powder
Olive oil
Salt and freshly milled
  black pepper

First pour boiling water over the tomatoes, leave them for a minute, then put them into cold water and slip the skins off. Halve them, discarding the seeds and chopping the flesh quite small.

Now soften the onion and garlic in a tablespoon of olive oil, then add the tomatoes, tomato purée, basil and chilli powder, seasoning at the same time. Stir well, then simmer gently for 15 minutes (covered), then for a further 10 or 15 minutes uncovered. Taste to check the seasoning when it's ready and either sieve the mixture or blend it in a liquidiser. Serve with meat loaf (see page 39) or plain chops or hamburgers.

Navarin of Lamb
(serves 4 or 6)

2½ lb middle neck of lamb,
  cut into pieces
Some dripping
2 tablespoons flour
1¾ pints hot water
1 level tablespoon
  tomato purée

1 clove garlic, crushed
6 small turnips, peeled
  and quartered
6 small thin carrots, cut
  into 1-inch lengths
12 small new potatoes,
  peeled

1 level teaspoon brown sugar	8 small onions, peeled and left whole
½ teaspoon mixed herbs	Salt and freshly milled black pepper

Begin by heating some dripping in a flameproof casserole. Season the meat then fry it in the hot fat till brown on all sides. Now sprinkle in the flour and cook, stirring gently all the time, to soak up the juices. Add the water, tomato purée, garlic and mixed herbs, bring slowly to the boil, giving another good stir, and simmer very gently for 45 minutes.

In the meantime fry the onions, turnips and carrots for 10 minutes and when the 45 minutes is up, add them to the casserole, bring again to simmering point, add the sugar, put a lid on and simmer very gently for a further 45 minutes.

New Potatoes with Mint and Chives
(serves 4)

1½ lb new potatoes	1 tablespoon fresh (or dried) chives, chopped
2 oz butter	
1 tablespoon fresh mint, chopped	Salt and freshly milled black pepper

Wash the new potatoes to remove any dirt, but do not peel. Then boil in salted water until the potatoes are cooked but still *firm* – do not overcook. Then add the butter, mint and chives to the saucepan, and toss the potatoes in the mixture until they are well coated. Season to taste and serve.

Fresh Salmon and Cucumber Mousse
(serves 4)

6 oz fresh cold salmon,
  cooked and finely
  mashed
3 level teaspoons
  powdered gelatine
¼ pint boiling water
¼ pint fresh single cream
The yolks and whites of
  2 eggs

1 level teaspoon paprika
1 tablespoon lemon juice
1 level teaspoon salt
2 tablespoons cucumber,
  peeled and chopped
  into smallish dice
A few thin slices
  cucumber

First of all bring the water to the boil in a saucepan,
gradually sprinkling in the gelatine and stirring vigor-
ously until it's dissolved. Now warm the cream slightly
and beat it into the egg yolks thoroughly. Next stir in
the dissolved gelatine and add the salt, paprika and
lemon juice.

Then the mixture should be allowed to get quite cold
and when it's just starting to set, stir in the mashed
salmon and cucumber. Beat the egg whites until stiff
and carefully fold them in. Spoon the mixture into four
glasses and chill thoroughly until firm. Just before serving decorate each one with thin slices of cucumber.

Mackerel with Green Gooseberry Sauce
(serves 2)

2 medium-sized fresh
  mackerel (ask the
  fishmonger to gut them
  and remove head and
  fins)
½ lb young gooseberries
½ oz butter

A little castor sugar (to
  taste)
The juice of 1 lemon
A little grated nutmeg
Olive oil
Salt and freshly milled
  black pepper

First prepare the sauce by washing the gooseberries (no need to top and tail them), and placing them in a small saucepan. Add enough water to cover and simmer gently until the gooseberries are cooked, about 6 to 10 minutes. Now drain the gooseberries and press the pulp through a sieve back into the saucepan, add a knob of butter and enough sugar to taste plus a little freshly grated nutmeg, and keep the sauce warm while preparing the fish.

Pre-heat the grill and line the pan with foil, then wash the mackerel and dry them thoroughly. Season inside and out with fresh lemon juice and salt and pepper, then place them on the grill-pan and score them lightly with two oblique cuts on both sides; brush the fish with olive oil and grill under a moderate heat until lightly browned. Turn the mackerel over, brush with oil again, brown on the other side, then serve immediately with the gooseberry sauce.

Beef Braised in White Wine
(serves 2)

1 lb chuck steak, cut into bite-sized cubes	1 dessertspoon flour
2 medium inions, roughly chopped	$\frac{1}{2}$ pint dry white wine
1 clove garlic, crushed	1 small strip orange peel (approx. 1 inch)
1 small sprig fresh thyme (or $\frac{1}{4}$ teaspoon dried)	Oil
1 bayleaf	Salt and freshly milled black pepper

Pre-heat the oven to gas mark 3, 325°F. Melt a little oil in a flameproof casserole and gently fry the onion and garlic in it for about 10 minutes, then turn the heat up a little and add the cubes of meat. (Keep them on the

59

move, with a wooden spoon, until they're nicely browned all over.) Now sprinkle in the flour and let that cook and soak up the juices, then gradually stir in the white wine.

Add the herbs and orange peel, season with salt and pepper, then cover with a lid and let it cook gently in the oven for about $2\frac{1}{2}$ hours or until the meat is tender. Alternatively it can be cooked on top of the stove – but keep your eye on it, stirring now and then to prevent it sticking.

Raspberry Shortcake
(serves 4 to 6)

1 lb raspberries (carefully picked over and washed)
8 oz plain flour
5 oz soft brown sugar

3 oz butter (room temperature)
1 level teaspoon baking powder
1 dessertspoon castor sugar

Pre-heat the oven to gas mark 4, 350°F. First of all arrange the prepared raspberries in a flameproof baking dish and sprinkle them with castor sugar. Then sift the flour and baking powder into a mixing bowl and lightly rub the butter into it until the mixture reaches a crumbly consistency.

Now mix in the soft brown sugar and sprinkle this mixture over the fruit – very lightly, without pressing down. Smooth the surface evenly, then bake in the oven for 30 to 40 minutes. Serve hot or cold with fresh whipped cream.

Plum and Soured Cream Flan
(serves 4 to 6)

6 oz sweet shortcrust
    pastry
1 lb dessert plums
2 5-oz cartons soured
    cream
1 oz castor sugar

3 egg yolks
½ teaspoon mixed spice
2 oz demarara sugar
1 teaspoon ground
    cinnamon

Pre-heat the oven, and a baking sheet, to gas mark 6, 400°F. Roll out the shortcrust pastry to line a 10-inch fluted flan tin, then halve the plums and remove the stones. Now beat the soured cream together with the castor sugar, egg yolks and mixed spice, then pour this mixture into the flan case and arrange the plums over the top (flat side up). Place the flan on the baking sheet and bake for 20 minutes.

Then mix the cinnamon with the demarara sugar and sprinkle it all over the top. Bake for a further 20 minutes, turning the heat right up to gas mark 8, 450°F, for the final 5 minutes so that the top can brown nicely. Serve warm or cold.

Wheatmeal Bread
(for 2 small or 1 large round cob loaf)

12 oz wheatmeal flour
4 oz plain flour
¼ oz lard
2 level teaspoons castor
    sugar
2 level teaspoons salt

2 level teaspoons dried
    yeast
½ pint water (hand-hot)
1 heaped tablespoon
    cracked wheat
A little oil

(Note: Use 85% wholemeal flour if wheatmeal is not
    available.)

Begin by placing a teaspoon of castor sugar in a small bowl, then measure the $\frac{1}{2}$ pint of water and pour about half of it onto the sugar. Stir until the sugar has dissolved, then sprinkle in 2 level teaspoons of dried yeast. Give the mixture a few quick stirs, then leave it for about 10 minutes so the yeast can dissolve and form a good frothy head.

While that's happening, place the flours in a large mixing bowl together with two level teaspoons of salt and a level teaspoon of castor sugar. Mix everything together thoroughly, then lightly rub in the $\frac{1}{4}$ oz of lard (which helps to keep the bread moist). Make a well in the centre of the dry ingredients and pour in the yeast mixture when it's ready, together with the rest of the measured water (always pour all liquid in at once, by the way).

Now start to mix with a large fork and finish off with your hands, mixing until you have a smooth dough that leaves the bowl clean (if it seems a little too dry, add a spot more water). Transfer the dough onto a lightly floured flat surface, and start to knead it.

All you do is stretch the dough, then fold it towards you, pushing it down then back away from you with the palm of your hand or your fist. Give the dough a quarter turn then repeat – as roughly as you like. Soon the dough will start to feel much firmer and more elastic. Give it about 6 to 10 minutes kneading altogether, then shape it into two neat rounds (or one large one if you like).

Place the dough on a slightly greased baking sheet, then brush the surface with some salted water (which helps to make them crisp when they're cooked). And sprinkle on some cracked wheat, if you have any. Now take a large polythene bag (a transparent pedal-bin liner is ideal for this), put a few drops of oil in it and rub it all round the inside of the bag to prevent the dough sticking to it. Place the baking sheet with the bread dough on it inside the bag, tie it loosely allowing room for expansion, and leave it in a warm place to rise.

Pre-heat the oven to gas mark 8, 450°F at this point (the baking sheet can be placed near, or on top of, the stove which is as good a place as any). In about 30 minutes the dough will have risen to about twice its original size, and to test if it's ready, touch it with your little finger – and if it feels very springy, it's ready.

Now remove the polythene bag, place the tray on the middle shelf of the pre-heated oven and bake the bread for about 20 to 30 minutes for small loaves, or 30 to 40 minutes for a large one.

When it's cooked it will feel hollow when tapped underneath. Put to cool on a wire tray, and then it's ready to be eaten.